*Destroyed Dresses*

Cara Brennan was born in Harrogate, North
Yorkshire, in 1990, and studied for an MA in
Creative Writing at Newcastle University. She
has worked for Flambard Press and *Mslexia*,
and more recently at Newcastle's Lit & Phil
library. She is a graduate of the Writing Squad.

Her poetry has been published in *Stanza
Stones: The Anthology,* and by *Ink, Sweat and
Tears, Dead Ink, The Cadaverine, Pomegranate,
Myths of the Near Future, NAWE* and *The Beat.
Destroyed Dresses* is Cara's debut pamphlet,
and was selected to be part of New Writing
North's 'Read Regional' campaign in 2013.

# Destroyed Dresses

## Cara Brennan

*Valley Press*

800452359

First published in 2012 by Valley Press
Woodend, The Crescent, Scarborough, YO11 2PW
www.valleypressuk.com

Reprinted in 2013

ISBN: 978-1-908853-07-3
Cat. no.: VP0037

A CIP record for this book is
available from the British Library

Printed and bound in Great Britain by
Volume Ltd., Reading, Berkshire

www.valleypressuk.com/authors/carabrennan

# Contents

## Acknowledgements

I would like to thank the editors of the following publications, where some of these poems have previously appeared: *Ink, Sweat and Tears*, *Myths of the Near Future*, *Pomegranate*, *Dead Ink*, *The Beat* and *Stanza Stones: The Anthology*.

I would also like to thank Steve Dearden and Danny Broderick of the Writing Squad, for their constant energy and enthusiasm for young writers; Sean O'Brien and Bill Herbert for their encouragement and feedback during my MA; the department of English at Newcastle University for awarding me a bursary for my MA; Caroline Grove who provided me with the amazing dress pattern packet which appears on the cover; Jamie McGarry at Valley Press for putting the book together; my fantastic editor Ellen Phethean; all my family and friends who have been so supportive and patient; and finally to my wonderful parents Chris and Rana who I could not have done it without.

*for Matt*

## Quilt

The October sun breeds
cataracts, the breeze
freezes my bones.

My neck is wool-deep in check;
it's hard to text
with mittens on.

It's not been this bright in weeks,
the glow shows glitter
in frost up the street.

The morning is a hot drink
in a cold glass, the nights are
drawing in.

We'll pull the blanket to the bed.
It's patchwork,
made from destroyed dresses.

I see one,
black with small blue birds,

their feathers shake
in the chill of my house, their beaks
are hurried applause.

## Fifth Birthday

In the mid-nineties the winters were long,
freezing, stagnant. It often snowed
in February, birthday white.
I watched the stretched flakes through
our goldfish-bowl window,
wearing my party dress;
pink and black check taffeta,
ruffled sleeves and hem.
The blizzard made Mum
pull me on the sledge, up the hill to school.
We left silver tracks in the snow.

## Bobble

We're at the top of The White Horse
looking for an edge to scatter Gamphy's ashes.
Beyond the cinder track and brittle fence
stands an airfield
where gliders impersonate curlews;
the wind will give them flight.

I am fearful.
My hair is plaited,
held with an orange bobble,
covered with scratchy fabric,
lace, a silk bow, pearls.
A gust may take it from me.

# Medusozoa

Clutching my skin, pin-spotted with fire,
I ran from the shore sobbing.

A jellyfish, litter from the escaping tide,
fluorescent plastic bag distended
with organs and air.

Everyone surrounded me
but her. Mum was napping in the blue tent,
her brain recoiling from unwelcome
growth. Flesh had turned to stone.

Stinging on the beach I shivered, flinched
at the vinegar stink.
If only I'd been back home
practising my strokes
in the swimming pool, her eyes
keeping me afloat.

The Wood Run

We built large fires each night to warn off the chill.
We'd go, after the beach, to Bluebell Wood for tinder;
I'd edge past nettles
and rabbits shaking with myxomatosis,
their lives as small as my own.

I saw a family of deer, coy amongst the dripping birches.
Dad told me not to get distracted, to drag twigs
up the domino steps, over the stile, through the field of
    untouched crops;
to the tents that diluted the grass to yellow beneath them.

## Pooh Sticks

Early evening, hair wet from the beach, curly
when the salt sinks in. We head to the wood.
The stone steps are slants, slippery with moss.

The bridge at the bottom of the slope
is copper with rust. I run behind my cousins,
search for the best twig.

We drop them into the flow,
watch them float downstream.
Crouching, peering through the railings,
my hair is the bridge.

## Nibbler

Nibbler rose from the ashes
of a Leeds annihilation.

We fetched him, five weeks old.
Meows, wet gasps through the window
like Cathy's to Heathcliff.

His green eyes, petrified,
they rolled as marbles.

Claws mirror my chipped nails,
he sleeps outside my bedroom door,
warm carpet, a bed softer than his first breath.

I trace his dreams in the ghost of trees,
overturned pushchairs, burnt-out cars.

## The Air Moves Other Things

The bus heaves past and in this autumn light
my shadow is a rabbit on a hook.

I follow it to Sandyford Racetrack.
I am looking for rats, in undergrowth.
They are fur-shakers, stirring
as the air moves other things; feathers,
broken umbrellas, plastic cups.

Paper leaves punctuate the hedge;
I remember the walk
back from town last week.
Four in the morning
a window lit in the tower block,
squares of confetti fell ahead of us.
*The Daily Sport* illuminated by street lamps,
flung from up high, a flock of bold
tabloid sequins.

## Bevelled Edge

Leaning over the glass,
with carburettor cleaner-
soaked cotton wool.
I'm dragging at the blemishes,
the streaks and drops.

This mirror is from the thirties
because of its edge.

Hanging above the sideboard
in our new living room
it looks the part, but changes
era with the things it frames.
Our paperback books, plant pots, speakers.

I gauge my quivering mouth,
imagine faces this glass has seen,
before the surface was tarnished,
before it was unusual.

Attic

The seams have been unpicked sharply,
unlike the soft print fingers leave
at the top of my legs. Threads are loose,
a flapper's edge or rug's frame. Old stitches
leave tiny holes in fabric, it breathes.

In my waking dream the dress is reincarnated,
worn by a spectre. Dragged
along the wet beach, the train kicks up
flecks of sand, leaves a fossil.

## Sequin Dress

You stole the mermaid's tail
used to distract distant sailors,
a patchwork of tiny mirrors
reflecting beams of light.

It creates shapes on the bedroom wall
as you dance under our paper lampshade.
You look beautiful, yet seldom pull on
your sequin gown.

Now that she swims with bare fins
and blushes behind rocks,
with peach flesh she must reach for stars.

## The Reference Room

I'm copying discoloured words
and breathing dust, waiting
for something to move me.
I'm told you can hear
the ghost turn pages.

I hear the wind.

I hear men sniff and
use their pens abruptly. I'm told
this is the warmest room
but I am cold;

breeze, breeze blowing.

This downbeat table is a good height
but the clock ticks loudly.
It traces the pace of my ink;
it pours old time down my back.

I consider the lore,

think of yellowing pages
held by ghosts.
The clock's rotating hands
become my pulse.

Freight Train

You wrote your name on a freight train,
sprayed a metallic scenario
over the heavy-haul snake, flecks
of paint, cracked scales.

Your tag raced the length of soundproof trees
like mute words in glass bottles,
jolted around blind corners;
young dancers in dark rooms.

You wrote your name on a freight train.
Two hundred miles of steel blazed,
friction flashing
small parts of your existence.

Tracking a life, the click-clack
of graffiti, high-speed calligraphy.

## Missing the Walk at Nab Hill

Sleek men stole copper from the train tracks.
Their sly pluckings leave my carriage stranded
just outside Alnwick.

I'm late into Howarth
so watch the hills from this hotel car park;
the splendour of their height,

trace the soft outline of them,
recall your frame.
The way you stretch on your side,

defy the fierce morning. The surface of these fells
is a fine layer of hair,
your chest is covered with similar moss.

Cairns are positioned like Jenga pieces,
they cleave the wind.

Cherry Beer

I would wait up for you. I'd wash my hair,
put the make-up on so it looked like
I wasn't wearing any but looked better
than wearing none and sit

on my bed reading, watching catch-up TV
until you texted 'hey! I'm outside x.'

That bit was never a surprise.
I'd trained myself to know
the sound, you getting out of a taxi;
an engine muted
a door slam
footsteps.
I couldn't be mad if you were late

we were so new
you weren't yet mine,
you changed my candlelit scowls
with cherry beer in bed.
We would familiarise our day
tearing wrappers from bottles,

alternate sips and kisses before dawn
where I would fold
the scrunched red paper into cranes
and hold them after you left.

We were so new
you weren't yet mine.

Wool, Skin, Fur

In my first year at University
I wore a red Duffel coat.
Bought when my loan came in
it kept me warm, muted homesickness.
The hood was thick – I wrapped myself,
muffled my tears.

In second year I had a sheepskin,
a friend had taken it
from the cloakroom of a club.
It had snowed all evening, we danced inside.
At four in the morning, seeing shapes,
the taxis stopped. I slept under it,
the house was freezing.

In third year I had fake-fur,
six pounds from Cancer Research.
I wore it on our cold first date, curled it up
into a pet when the house was empty.
Plants grew through the kitchen door:
I was an animal in a strange habitat.

This year my coat is woollen, beige,
my room is warmer because it's not just mine;
we share everything. I see your coats now;
the suede bomber, denim jacket with cord trim,
how they hang with mine, against the door.

## Pattern

In October I unfolded the map of you.
A paper pattern, limbs traced,
snipped to create your outline.

I started with the hand that clutched
cigarettes, carefully stirred
unusual drinks.

There was a dotted line
where I folded your mouth
on a neglected sofa. We measured
the length of my room in lips,
tongues, teeth.
I cut darts for your eyes,
the template of your face.
Your hair was thick back then;
I've trimmed it down to size.

The trickiest outline was your chest;
pulsing, difficult
to give it a smooth edge.
I left it for a while,
pinned the rest of you to flesh –
tidied your heartbeat away.

December, my hands are steadier;
you are almost ready to wear.
I retrieve the pieces; tack your torso,
calm, waiting to be stitched.